Doodle Yourself Happy

DOODLE YOURSELF HAPPY

A Therapeutic Doodling Workbook for Children Who Feel Sad or Low

TANJA SHARPE

Foreword by Eve Sharpe
Illustrated by Tanja Sharpe

Jessica Kingsley Publishers
London and Philadelphia

First published in Great Britain in 2024 by Jessica Kingsley Publishers
An imprint of John Murray Press

1

Copyright © Tanja Sharpe 2024
Foreword copyright © Eve Sharpe 2024

Front cover image source: Tanja Sharpe.

The fonts, layout and overall design of this book have been prepared according to dyslexia-friendly
principles. At JKP we aim to make our books' content accessible to as many readers as possible.

A CIP catalogue record for this title is available from the British Library and the Library of Congress

ISBN 978 1 83997 622 3
eISBN 978 1 83997 623 0

Printed and bound in Great Britain by Bell & Bain Limited

Jessica Kingsley Publishers' policy is to use papers that are natural, renewable and recyclable
products and made from wood grown in sustainable forests. The logging and manufacturing
processes are expected to conform to the environmental regulations of the country of origin.

Jessica Kingsley Publishers
Carmelite House
50 Victoria Embankment
London EC4Y 0DZ

www.jkp.com

John Murray Press
Part of Hodder & Stoughton Limited
An Hachette UK Company

Contents

Foreword

As a therapist, fellow doodler and counsellor, I know that creativity and doodling offer a number of physical and psychological benefits for growing minds. Add an increase in happy hormones to the mix and you create a recipe that has the potential to have a huge impact on the development of the growing brain.

Feeling good and feeling happy are not dependent on what happens to us, but on how we feel about what happens to us and how we behave as a result of how we think. Therapeutic doodling and the pages before you are a brilliant reflection of the magic that can happen when we allow those conscious or unconscious thoughts to flow, without judgement or criticism but instead with curiosity and an inquisitive mind.

In my experience, young people who spend time doodling are often inherently creative and have strong focus and attention skills. They are often great problem solvers and multi-taskers and learn to express and regulate emotions well. For this reason, encouraging creativity and an awareness around happiness habits can be incredibly beneficial for young minds, helping to develop the skills and abilities to reduce stress, manage anxiety and gain deeper control and awareness in their ever-changing lives.

I am both excited and honoured to be able to introduce this book *Doodle Yourself Happy*. I am incredibly proud of the amazing work Tanja is doing in highlighting the therapeutic benefits of doodling, both because she is my sister, but also because, in my role as a *Happiness for No Reason Facilitator* with a passion for helping clients to grow happiness within their own lives, I see the benefits her work brings.

I see time and time again the powerful change that can come from the ebb and flow of creatively weaving your pen across paper, allowing your internal thoughts, feelings and emotions to pour out and to mirror back to you all that has been locked away inside. Even the simple task of drawing a happy smiley face and showing it to the person across the room can bring joy, without the use of a single word.

Doodling is so much more than markings on paper or mindless scribbles we create without thought. In fact, we know that the act of doodling activates the reward pathways in our brain. Therefore, doodling is not only good for our minds, thoughts and emotions, but it physically releases the endorphins that make us feel good too. It can be a calming and creative way to express yourself and reduce stress, worry and anxiety.

As a child, Tanja was never far from a pen and piece of paper and could often be found tucked away in a corner doodling away in her books. As children we were encouraged to fill our books with art and doodles as a way to keep us engaged in lessons and grow our creativity alongside our learning practices. I have vivid memories of the vines and flowers Tanja would wrap around her pages and the many doodles she created while listening to her teachers. Her books and writing have always been full of characters and expressive doodles as she weaves stories and creates magic throughout the pages.

As she grew older the art of doodling continued, thoughts and emotions etched into paper with creative expression, filling books and journals with cylindrical, diagonal and spherical shapes, words and illusions to give shape and form to all that was happening inside of her. She would spend hours on beaches creating shapes and weaving stories in and out of the sand in mindful moments of curiosity.

Still, to this day, you will see Tanja's hand dancing across pages doodling as she works, thinks, makes calls or comes up with new ideas around the office. Her many doodled characters and stories bring magic into our days and bring smiles to the faces of all those who pop in to see us. This magic continues to flow throughout these pages and Tanja's work is a reflection of her passion, effort and lifetime dedication to creativity and the incredible benefits these simple patterns can have in all areas of our lives.

Over the years Tanja has taken her love and passion for doodling and helping others even further. As the founder of a global therapeutic community, Creative Counsellors, Tanja has trained thousands of counsellors, therapists, parents and children in the art of creativity. Along the way we have used Tanja's incredible knowledge of doodling throughout the workshops and courses we have run for organizations, charities and businesses around the world.

This next book in Tanja's book series – *Doodle Yourself Happy* – has a much-needed focus on happiness at a time where the world faces significant challenges. I hope that you will love the journey that the character Mello takes you on as you explore these pages with young people.

Eve Sharpe
Counsellor, Coach and Certified Happy for No Reason Trainer
www.creativecounsellors.org

For the Doodlers, Daydreamers and Awesome Readers (That's You!)

(Maybe you could get a little help from an adult to read this bit if you need it!)

Hi! I'm Tanja and I'm really happy that you found this book. In my job as a counsellor, I help people to find their happiness and to grow more of it through counselling, coaching and creative workshops. Happiness is something that we don't often hear people talking about in everyday life and yet it's something that is so important to us, our minds and our bodies.

We often spend more time worrying about things than we do on growing our happiness and that's what we need to be able to feel good about ourselves and our life.

When we plant a new garden there are some things that we need to do to help that garden grow. We need to plan the space for the garden, pick some seeds, dig a little home for them, wrap them in soil, water them, treat them gently, keep checking on them, give them a little stability if they begin to grow all wobbly, feed them, remove any pesky snails, slugs and bugs and give them sunlight.

Growing our own happiness is like planting a garden. We need to take some time and space to practise happiness, we need to pick some ways that we might do this, especially the stuff that we like that feels good. We need to think of it like planting new happiness seeds in our thoughts, feeding and nurturing them with activities, healthy food and exercise.

When our thoughts become a little wobbly and we have stress or feel down, then we need to help by removing those pesky thoughts that are causing those feelings. It's also important for us to have sunlight, fresh air and time in nature.

Even when we take care of our happiness there will be days when we feel low or sad and this is normal but sometimes it can help to speak to someone that you trust for help. This might be your parent, a teacher, an older brother or even a friend's parent. If you want to talk to someone for help on the phone, then you can also call Childline on 0800 1111 to speak with a friendly adult who cares about your feelings. There are lots of places to find support if you need it.

As you work through this doodle book, know that you are planting new seeds for happiness that you can grow and feed and nurture!

Brain science (the awesome stuff that makes happiness work)

Your brain is full of chemicals that it releases every day into your body. This affects you in lots of different ways. Some of those chemicals are feel-good chemicals and if we practise growing happiness then we are helping our brain to boost more of those feel-good chemicals which then helps us in lots of ways. Imagine that by doodling your way through this book you are being a best friend to your brain and your brain is being a best friend to you!

Let's explore what we mean by 'feel-good chemicals'.

Dopamine

Helps us to feel motivated. If we don't have enough of it, we can struggle with our attention, learning, movement and sleep. We can boost our dopamine levels by getting a good amount of sleep, celebrating when we achieve things and exercising. We will do lots of celebrating as we doodle our way through this book and focus on how we can get more sleep and move more!

Endorphins

Help us to feel more energized, less stressed and in a happy mood. We can boost our endorphins when we exercise and laugh more. So, in this book, we will look at ways that we can bring more laughter into our lives!

Oxytocin

Helps us to feel loved and connected with other people. I call this the cuddle hormone because we release oxytocin when we cuddle someone we love. There are lots of oxytocin boosting doodles in this book!

Serotonin

Helps to boost our mood. When we practise being kind to others or being thankful for what we have, we can boost our serotonin. Vitamin D from sunshine can also help to boost serotonin.

Fun fact: Your brain can't tell the difference between what is real or what is imaginary. This is why you can get so excited when you play an exciting game and feel as though you are actually there in real life. In this doodle book, we will be using our imaginations to boost our serotonin.

The amygdala

Also known as 'your reptilian brain'. If we get scared or anxious, it works quickly to keep us safe by causing us to freeze, fight or run. Sometimes our brain can work too hard on keeping us safe and so we can get nervous or anxious even when we don't need to be. You can help the brain to feel safer and happier by doing more of the things that you love to do and that help you to feel calm, like doodling!

The hippocampus

This is where we store our memories. In this book, we will explore your happy memories to help boost your feel-good chemicals.

The prefrontal cortex

This is the part of the brain that helps us with willpower and creating new healthy habits. Did you know that some people believe that it takes 21 days to grow a new habit? When we are adventurous, curious, playful and have fun we can change our brain to be happier and this is called neuroplasticity! Let's create new happiness habits together!

Happiness is one of many emotions

Happiness is one of many emotions that we can feel. Emotions like sadness, excitement and worry flow through us every day like a river, but because feelings like worry feel so big and overwhelming, our brain and our body tend to dwell on them more. So, happiness is often left behind, until we notice it and begin to focus on growing more of it.

Happiness lives inside every one of us. Some people describe it as that feeling when you laugh at something funny or get excited about a new game coming out. I like to describe it as an everyday feeling of calm, warmth in my heart and joy at the littlest things. Like when I get to drink a hot chocolate with marshmallows, or a rainbow appears after the rain, or when someone I love gets good news.

It can be that feeling I get in my shoulders that feels warm and when my lips begin to curl into a smile. Many of us can feel happiness in our body as well as think it in our mind.

For you, happiness might feel like something totally different. Maybe we could practise for a quick moment and see if we can find your happiness starting point now? (Maybe an adult could read this bit to you while you close your eyes?)

Practise with me!

Close your eyes and think of something that makes you smile. Something that you really like and helps you to feel good. Can you think of that? Notice what you are feeling in your body and if your face changes. Do you feel any temperature changes or maybe notice your body relaxing a little? What else do you notice? Do you get a feeling in your stomach or your legs maybe?

How easy was that to think of? How happy did you feel? Mark that here by circling a number from 1–5 with 1 not feeling very happy at all and 5 feeling really, really, really happy. What number feels right for you?

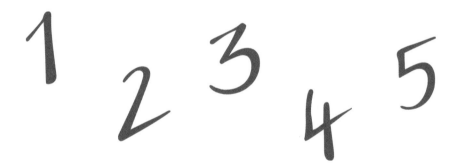

It's ok if that was harder than you thought it would be. Some people can think of something that makes them happy really easily and some people take time to grow happiness inside them. Some people feel happiness in their body and some people don't. There is no right or wrong way of feeling happy and I know that you will find your own unique way.

Life can feel hard and there are so many pressures to do well at school, to make friends and to always be doing your best.

This book is a little break from that. This book could be your daily break from worry, sadness and stress. You can spend time doodling, drawing and creating your way to more happiness.

You see, happiness actually takes practice! My friend used to say 'where your attention goes, that garden grows', and so for our happiness to grow we need to take some time to water and feed it with feel-good things.

This book has 50 different doodle sheets that can help you to do that and all with a little help from Mello!

Mello is one of the happiest characters I know and is relaxed, adventurous and brave. You will notice that Mello likes to go on adventures to find more happiness so that it can be shared with the world. Mello knows that the happier we are, the more we can share it to inspire others to be happier too.

What will we be doing?

Doodling/drawing

Doodling is when you draw shapes, squiggles, lines and patterns on the page. These can be any shapes and any colours. Maybe you feel like filling a whole page with stars or swirly lines. It can feel really relaxing to take some time to get lost in a page of squiggles, so when you are drawing in this book, have some fun and remember that there is no wrong or right way to doodle. You can add anything you like anywhere you like.

Zentangles

Zentangles are when you fill a shape with lots of doodles. So smaller doodles inside of a shape. The more you focus on them the more relaxed you could feel because your mind can't think of anything else but what you are doing now in this moment. It's a great way to let go of any stress and worries and to grow more happiness.

Writing

On some of the pages there may be some boxes and spaces to add your own words and thoughts. Writing can help you to clear your busy mind. It is also a great way to add your own sparkly touch to any of the doodles in this book. You don't need to only write in the boxes though. You can write anywhere you like!

Art

On any of the pages you can add anything you like! You can add collages, photos, paints, stickers or whatever makes you happy! This is your book, and you make the rules!

A Message for Your Parents, Carers and Helpers

(Share this bit with a trusted adult.)

There is so much stress placed on young people to perform and do well in life and this is ever increasing. On top of this, there is the added stress of social media, navigating friendships and the physical and emotional demand of living an online life.

Young people are struggling more and more with mental health and wellbeing, and you can be an incredible support system for them, gently guiding, nudging and promoting happiness habits that last.

You can help by:

- Growing happiness habits within yourself and modelling this for young people
- Expressing emotions when you feel them so young people know that they can too
- Modelling healthy boundaries and talking with young people about their own boundaries
- Making dedicated time to connect with the young people around you to talk about their life

- Responding with compassionate and caring body language
- Avoiding trying to fix a problem for a young person and instead holding space to talk and explore ways that the young person can problem solve for themself
- Acknowledging when they are trying and doing their best
- Complimenting young people on their humour, their kindness, who they are as a person and their individual uniqueness rather than the way that they look
- Modelling a healthy relationship with food
- Encouraging outdoor time in nature to help young people to destress, reground and discharge nervous energy
- Taking time to doodle and practise creativity for relaxation, confidence building and connection. Maybe you can support their journey through this book! This book can support young people as they grow up, empowering them with happiness habits to take into their teens and adult life.

The exercises, thoughts, nudges and doodles in this book are inspired by a range of therapeutic approaches which help to focus on cultivating happiness. Some of these include:

Behavioural activation
Behavioural activation is based on the idea that we can do things that feel good to change our mood and move from a place of feeling down or anxious to a place of feeling relaxed, positive or happy. We have the power to change the way that we feel and, in this book, we will focus on exercises and simple doodles which can help us to do this.

Mindfulness

Mindfulness can help us to slow things down, to clear our busy mind of overwhelming thoughts and to focus on things that help us to release stuck emotions and relax our bodies and minds. Often anxiety, worrying, feeling down and stress are due to an overactive mind focusing on things that don't feel great. We include mindfulness-based doodles in this book to help young people to focus on things that can feel good.

Cognitive Behavioural Therapy (CBT)

CBT helps us to understand that our thoughts have an impact on our emotions, our emotions have an impact on our body and how we feel physically, and this has an impact on our choices and our actions. For example, if I think that I am terrible at running and will be fearful of falling at my next race (thoughts), then I will feel anxious about racing (emotions), my heart might begin to speed up and I may feel nauseous while thinking about this (body) and I might avoid going to races altogether (choices and actions).

The exercises in this book help us to focus on things that we can control, while building strength and resilience skills. This in turn can help to create new neural pathways in the brain so it is wired for positive and loving connection and thoughts.

Positive Psychology

Positive Psychology helps us to focus on the good stuff, the positive events and memories in life where we feel or felt happiness, joy, love and connection to others. This also helps us to grow compassion, gratitude and resilience which boosts our emotional strength and confidence. This has an overall positive effect on our lives.

Happy Word Map

What does happy mean to you? On this doodle page, there are some words that people often pick to mean happiness for them. Do you have a different word or even words? Some other words could be laughing, warm, smiley or fun. Or maybe you have your own word like flubbering, which is Mello's favourite and means that good feeling that you get when you get home from school and can just throw yourself on the couch and flubber!

ACTION: Circle the words that feel happy for you and add your own words. You can see that I have begun to add some Zentangle doodles to the H in Happy and you can add your own Zentangles, colours or anything else that you like. Now you know your own unique happiness word map.

Chilled

Ok

Giggly

Excited

Peaceful

Joyful

Relaxed

2

Express Yourself

What colour would your happy be? Maybe it's a mix of blues and greens or bright pinks and purples. Maybe you think of happiness like sunshine and would choose yellows and oranges. This graffiti wall is waiting for your happy colour explosion. You could use paints, doodle with bright pens, crayons, chalks or anything you like to create your colour explosion.

ACTION: Choose colours that represent your happy and add them to the graffiti wall. You could create any shape that you like. Now you know what colours mean happy for you! Also, did you notice Mello hanging out somewhere in the wall?

3

Colour Bubbling

We can use our imagination to boost our feel-good chemicals. Now you know what happiness means to you and what colours represent your happy, you can imagine surrounding yourself in these colours and breathing them in.

As your body fills up with these colours, imagine breathing out all the stuff that you don't like to feel, imagine all the stress and worries just gently floating out of your body. You can add anything else you like to your imaginary colour bubble, like sprinkling glitter, shining stars or even sounds like laughter! How different do you feel now?

ACTION: There is a space next to Mello for you to doodle yourself in your own colour bubble and add anything you like. Remember to add any words, colours, glitter or anything else that you would like.

4

Protect Your Peace

Sometimes people aren't kind or caring towards us. This can happen in places like at school, online in your games or at the park with your friends and it can help to have a way to protect your peace. This means growing a strong shield that you can use when you need it most. Our imaginations can help us with this!

Now that you have a protective colour bubble, you can imagine surrounding yourself in this bubble whenever you feel like you need a little boost of something that feels good. Imagine any unkind words, actions or thoughts from other people bouncing off your bubble. Kind of like a super-power. This way you can protect your peace!

ACTION: In this doodle box, draw yourself in a super-power pose! What might you need? A cape, a magic spell? Mello is cheering you on! Notice how any words from others are bouncing off the bubble. You can choose what you allow inside your bubble!

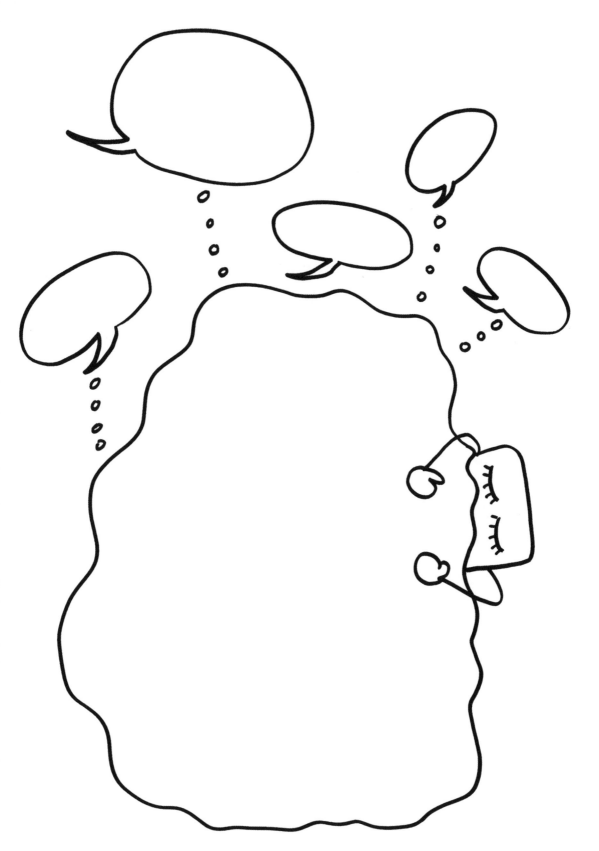

5

My Best Day Ever

What was your best day ever? Maybe you got to visit someone or went to the beach with your dog. Remembering these times can help to boost feel-good chemicals in our body and our brain. What was the best day ever for you? If you haven't had your best day ever, then maybe you could imagine what your best day ever could look like here.

ACTION: Write the title of your best day ever in the box with Mello and then create your memory. You can do this in words or doodles, whatever feels good for you.

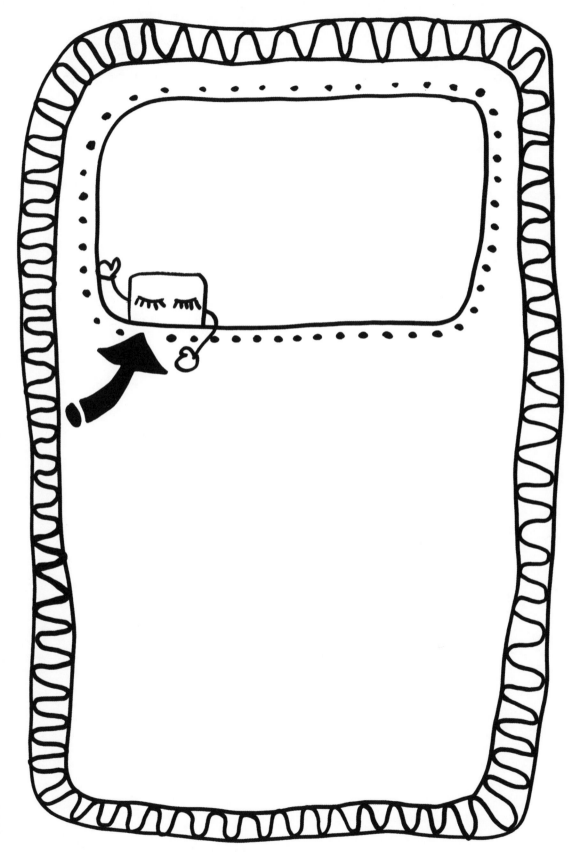

6

Cosy Moments

What helps you to feel relaxed at night when you get ready for sleep? Creating some cosy moments before sleep can really help our minds to relax. When our minds relax, our bodies can too, and we can forget about the things that can be worrying or stressing us out.

Did you know that bats like to wrap their wings around them when they go to sleep to keep themselves warm and cosy? What cosy moments could help you to feel more relaxed? Maybe wrapping yourself in a warm blanket, reading something or listening to a sleep story?

ACTION: Doodle something to keep Mello warm and relaxed. What could that be? Doodle the things that help you to feel relaxed and warm before bed.

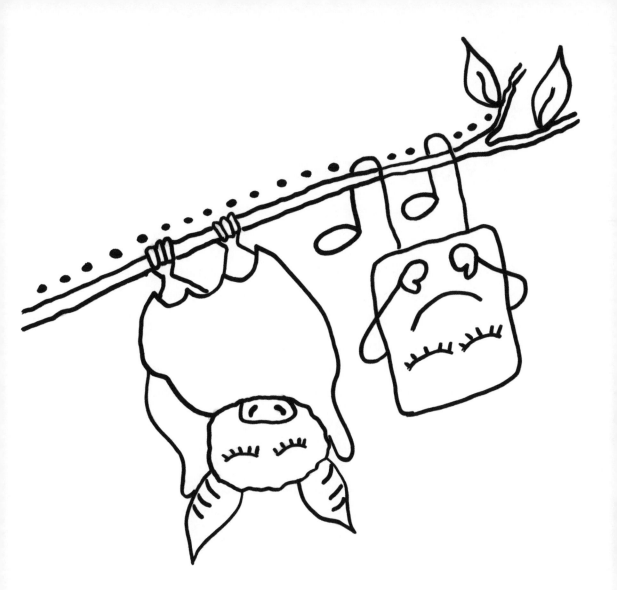

Ray of Sunshine

Have you ever heard the phrase 'a ray of sunshine'? It means someone who makes other people feel happy even in difficult situations. Mello has a best friend called Ray. Ray helps Mello to laugh and have fun even when things don't feel so good. It can be important to have people in your life who help you to feel like you have your own ray of sunshine when you need it.

ACTION: Write, doodle or create your own ray of sunshine on this page. Who are they? How do they help you? Add your own colours, squiggles, shapes and doodles to brighten up this page.

8

Grow Your Spark

We can grow happy feelings even when things feel tough, and it can all start with a little spark.

Using one of your happy words from your Happy Word Map, imagine that this word was a little spark of colour in your stomach. Now imagine that it grew brighter and brighter and bigger and bigger until it took over your whole stomach. Now imagine that this spark grew so big that it filled your whole body. Then it grew even more. It grew so big that it filled your whole room and then your whole house and then the whole street. Now it's so big that it's starting to fill the whole of planet earth!

Imagine how much wonderful feel-good energy you can share with the whole world. When we share our happiness, we can inspire other people to feel more happiness too. You could be the spark that changes the world!

ACTION: Doodle, draw and create your spark growing on this page. What colours will you choose? What shape is your spark and what else do you want to add?

9

Five Things You Love

The more we focus on the stuff that we love and appreciate, the more we feel good inside because we are focusing on and growing more happy feelings. Appreciation helps us to see the good parts of our life even when things feel like a struggle. We can appreciate a warm bath, a cool drink, someone doing something nice for us, our comfy pillow or a million other things.

If you begin to focus on the things you appreciate every day, you will develop positive connections in your brain and get even better at seeing the great things in your life.

ACTION: On this page, doodle five things that you love and appreciate in your life. These could be people, places, pets or anything that you want to add here.

You Are a Gift

We all have gifts that we bring to the world. Yours might be your funny sense of humour, or your caring nature to help others. Maybe you like to cook and share food with your family or play football in a team.

Your gifts become your strengths and sharing your gifts helps others to feel good too. When others feel good because of your kindness then your brain also releases feel-good chemicals. You might hear me say this a few times in this book because it's so important! Mello likes to be on a team and his gift in this doodle is to thank you for all that you are doing to share your gifts with the world.

ACTION: Doodle what gifts you are sharing with the world. You can do this in words, drawings or any way that you like. Like smiling at a stranger when you take a walk or giving a hug to someone.

11

Your Best Moves

When you spend a lot of time sitting or not moving enough your body can become tired and you can experience headaches, body pains and sometimes feel a bit down and anxious too. Movement, dance and exercise can help to boost your feel-good chemicals as well as lift your mood. Moving more can help you to sleep better, think better, relax more and feel a lot happier and lighter.

ACTION: Put on your favourite song and show the world your best moves. On this doodle, add colours, shapes and words to represent how it makes you feel to move more!

12

LOL

Laughing is the fastest way to help flip your mood and create feelings of happiness. When we laugh it strengthens our immune system (that part of us that keeps us healthy and well). Laughing can also pick your mood up when you are feeling down and it can help to relax your body.

ACTION: Can you remember the last time you laughed? What makes you laugh? Maybe it's funny videos on YouTube or seeing someone do something funny. Doodle all the things that make you laugh and brighten up the page with anything that feels good to you.

13

Happy Pets

Spending time with our pets can help us to feel good. This is because of those warm cuddles, their loving personalities and playful energy. Do you enjoy spending time with animals? Do they make you smile? Or maybe they fill you with good feelings? Do you feel warmer in your body? Pets can help to lower our stress feelings and other emotions that can feel tough, like anger.

ACTION: On this page I have begun to doodle some playful pets. Add your own and fill the page with wonderful and magical creatures. You can add your own real life pets or imaginary ones that you create.

14

Slow Things Down

We spend so much time rushing around in our lives that sometimes we can feel like life is set to fast-forward. It can help to be a little bit like a snail sometimes and to slow down a little to notice all the good things in the world around us.

Maybe the smell of something that you like or the colours in the sky. Maybe even the coolness of the rain on your face or the crack that a stick makes when you step on it. The world is full of awesome things to see and notice when we slow down a little.

ACTION: Practise slowing down and noticing what's around you. Doodle what you see, feel, hear and notice on this page. Then fill it with as many doodles as you like!

51

15

Stretch It Out

Sometimes we can stay stuck in one position for too long and this can cause our bodies to get tight and painful. Maybe you are sitting too much and get a sore neck or a headache. It can help to take some time to stretch your body and move it to release any trapped feelings or tight muscles.

ACTION: Find a space that you can move around in. Begin to stretch your body in as many ways as you would like to. Your body can talk to you and be your guide. Maybe reach for the sky or touch your toes. Reach your arms out and imagine that they were stretching from one side of the world to the other.

How good does it feel to stretch out those muscles? Doodle some of your favourite stretches on this sheet and how moving makes you feel as a reminder to keep stretching.

16

Wobbled

We will all have days where we feel like things are too much and we become wobbled. Maybe you are feeling like you have too much to do, or you have had an argument with someone. This is normal and even though things feel hard right now in this moment, it will change. Everything we feel is temporary and it changes. That is why it's important to practise growing happiness.

So, if you catch yourself feeling wobbled, remember that you can change your emotions. You can focus on something that feels good in the moment and flip your emotions so that you feel steady again.

ACTION: Mello's feeling wobbled. He has too many things that he is trying to balance and feels like he might come crashing down. Do you ever feel like that? When you are ready, flip the page and help him to balance by doodling something for his other leg to balance on. What could this be? What do you need when you feel wobbled? When he is balanced on two legs and holding an apple, things feel lighter and look different. Add any thoughts and feelings that you need to flip here to feel lighter about them. The more you practise flipping the easier it becomes.

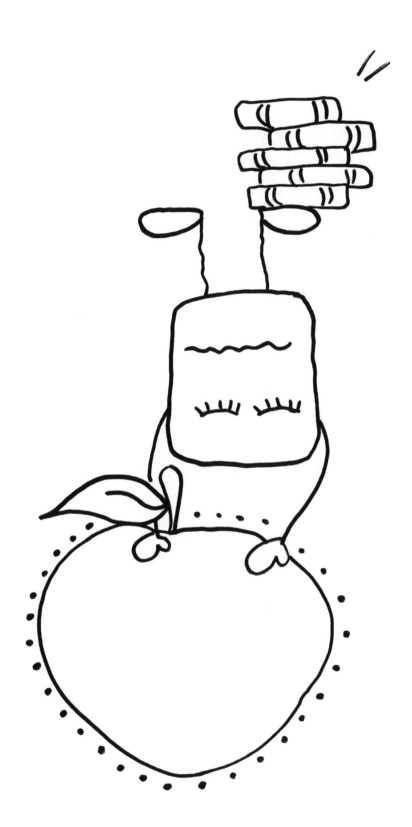

17

Find Your Own Style

There are so many people telling us how we should dress, speak and look, but what's more important is how you feel and how you express your own style in the world. When you find your own style and like what you wear and who you are, then you are helping your brain and your body to be more comfortable with who you really are. Celebrating all the amazing differences that we all have and being unique is what makes the world the wonderful place that it is!

ACTION: In this doodle express yourself by playing with different styles. What would be your dream outfit? What would be your dream hairstyle? What colours would you wear? What else would you do to express who you are in the world? Add anything that helps you to do this to the doodle. You could even cut out images from magazines or find them online to show who you really are.

18

Marshmallowed

This is one of Mello's favourite ways to be! Of course, being a marshmallow has its advantages! Being marshmallowed is like peaceful happiness, when you feel so relaxed that you sink into your sofa or flop over your chair in your room and just feel amaaaaaaazing! Finding your own way to feel marshmallowed can help to grow peaceful happiness, especially if you are feeling stressed or worrying about something.

ACTION: (It could be helpful to get someone to read this to you.)

Make yourself really comfortable. Maybe you need to wrap yourself in a blanket or kick your shoes off and jump on your bed for this cosy you-time. Now close your eyes and imagine that you are floating on the softest and most comfortable cloud. This cloud is so fluffy that you sink into it and it feels so good.

Now imagine that your whole body begins to feel as melty and soft as a marshmallow. Every one of your muscles relaxing, sinking more and more into that soft fluffy cloud. Notice how relaxed you feel. When you are ready, doodle colours, words, shapes and feelings.

19

Ten Kind Acts

Have you ever been around someone who just started laughing and you didn't know why but it made you laugh too? This is because when we see other people have an emotion it can activate or start that emotion in us too. So, when we are kind to others and we help to create some happiness in them, then this can create happiness in us too! We can be kind to others simply by smiling at someone, opening a door for someone, saying thank you or something nice about someone. There are so many ways that we can be kind to others.

ACTION: Doodle 10 ways that you can show kindness and share some of that happiness that you are growing inside of you with others. Notice how it feels to be kind to others.

20

Thought Bubbles

Take a minute to imagine sending your thoughts out of your mind and into the sky in bubbles. Some of your thoughts might feel great and some might not feel so good and that's ok. We all have thousands of thoughts every day. Some we will remember and some we won't, but it can be helpful to take some time to clear your mind of any thoughts you are having so that you have some space to grow a little happiness.

ACTION: Fill these bubbles with any thoughts that you are having now in this moment. Doodle some more bubbles and fill your page. These can be random thoughts like 'blue squishy ice-cream' or memories or anything else that you are thinking about. Imagine them floating away into the sky until you can't see them any more.

21

Word Power

What you say leaves your body as an energy bolt. The sound travels into the world. The words you say matter. Science shows that if you say positive things out loud to yourself or others that you can grow some powerful energy around these words. For example, if you think 'I did awesome today' this is great and really helpful. If you also say it or even shout it out loud: 'I DID AWESOME!', that's like sending a boomerang of your awesome voice out into the world which comes back to you and boosts your energy.

ACTION: Write down three positive things about you (get some help from someone if you need some inspiration) and then say, sing or shout these out loud! Remember that when you throw a boomerang you need to put your energy into it, so really throw that amazing voice of yours out there! When you do this, notice how it can instantly boost your happy energy!

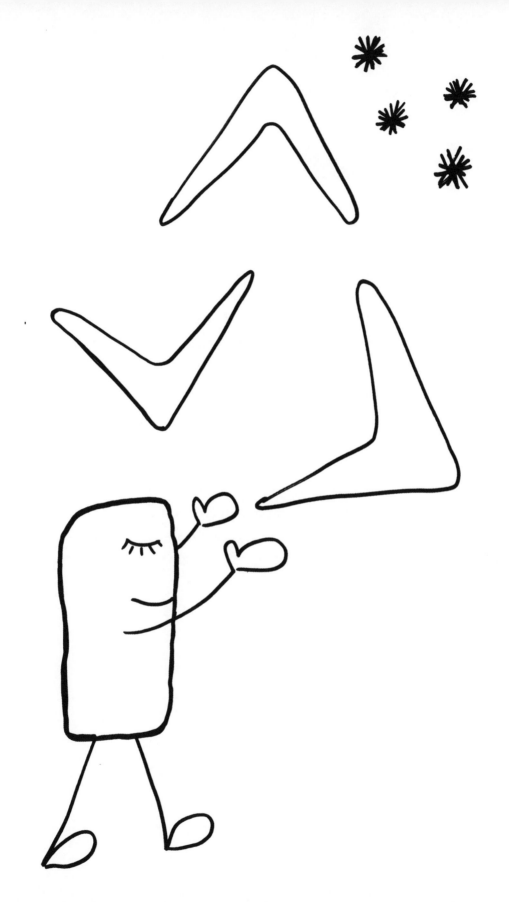

65

22

Zentangled

A Zentangle a day keeps stress away. An American study showed that if you doodle Zentangles for 80 minutes a week, this helps you to feel less anxious and happier.[1] The cool thing is you just need some paper and some pens to get started. Find a comfy place to relax and maybe even put on some of your favourite music to help.

ACTION: I have started to add some shapes to this doodle with plenty of space for you to add your own. Once you have your shapes, you can begin to fill them with lots of squiggles, patterns, colours, words or anything that you would like to. Mello isn't here so maybe you could add him if you want to. He makes a great shape for Zentangles!

23

Nature Gatherers

Have you heard of the fancy word 'biophilia'? This word was invented by a man called Erich Fromm and he found that all humans love to be connected to nature. It helps us to balance our energy and to feel good.

It's like that feeling when you get to lie in your garden with the warm sun on your face, or that cold splash of water when you go for a swim in nature. When we are in nature, we can appreciate how amazing our world is and it helps to relax our bodies and our minds.

ACTION: Take some time outside. Notice all the sounds, the colours, the smells and how the ground feels under your feet. What patterns do you find in nature? Doodle what you find and how you feel on this sheet. Was there something that you noticed that you haven't noticed before?

24

Your Inside Weather

It's easy to see what the weather is like when we look outside the window, but have you ever noticed how your feelings and emotions can feel like inside weather? Sometimes we can feel as angry as a tornado in our stomachs or as fierce as a fire when something doesn't feel fair. Maybe we can feel as sad as a waterfall in our eyes or as excited as a thunderstorm in our head.

ACTION: In this box doodle your inside weather right now. Then think of all the ways that emotions can be like weather for you. What weather would your anger be? What weather would your happiness be?

When you begin to feel these emotions in the future you can remind yourself that your emotions and your feelings are like weather. They change all the time. They float in and float away again, just like clouds. This is why we have to practise growing the happy weather that we want to see!

25

Take a Break

Sometimes we can be so busy studying or thinking about things that we become exhausted. We can then feel anxious, stressed or another emotion that doesn't feel so good.

Did you know that your brain can be scanned using an fMRI machine? This clever machine can see which parts of your brain are lighting up in different colours based on what you are doing. When you are resting, letting your mind wander or taking a break it is called 'default mode'. Default mode helps you to think about the past and your memories, to daydream or think about the future adventures you might have and other things in your life. It's important to have breaks to have a healthy brain and body.

ACTION: Take a break right now from anything that you are doing. Maybe let your mind wander or simply watch the clouds floating by. Doodle what it feels like to take a break. Maybe doodle what you see.

26

Hold Someone in Your Heart

Is there someone in your life that you would like to send an extra burst of loving and feel-good energy to? Maybe your parent, a friend, someone at school or even your pet? Remember your brain doesn't know the difference between thinking about holding someone in your heart and really holding them in your heart. So, it has the same effect on your brain and body. This is called visualization and it means to visualize or imagine something. You can get a big feel-good boost from sharing loving energy with others.

ACTION: Doodle a person or maybe a few people in your heart that you want to send loving energy to. Imagine that energy flowing like a river from your heart to them, surrounding them with your loving energy. Doesn't that feel good?

27

Bang a Drum! Let It All Out!

We all have emotions and feelings that can build up inside us. Sometimes it can help to find a way to let it all out. If you have a drum like the djembe, which is a small African drum that you play with both hands, then you can close your eyes and make your own rhythms. Maybe you need some gentle and relaxing sounds or maybe you need some faster and stronger sounds.

If you don't have a drum then you can use an air drum, pretending that you are playing drums to your favourite songs in the air around you. Jump around and let any thoughts and emotions that are stuck in your brain and body out into the air while you are drumming, adding some dance, singing or anything else that feels good.

ACTION: Imagine that you have a set of drums or a djembe drum. Play a song that you want to drum along to and begin to air drum. Move as much as you like; this is your time to let it all out. Doodle what it was like for you to drum and let it all out. Maybe add colours, shapes, Zentangles or anything else that you want to add here.

28

Try Something New

Trying something new can take courage. Often we can feel excited and anxious at the same time. In this doodle Mello is trying paddleboarding. He starts off being so nervous that his legs are shaking but then he remembers that he has tried new things before and sometimes forgets just how much courage and bravery he has. No matter what happens, when he tries something new, he always learns something new and knows that he is strong and able to face any challenges in his life.

ACTION: What new things have you tried? What would you like to try? Who do you need to help you to try these new things? Doodle all your ideas on the sheet. As always, add any colours, words, patterns and shapes that you like.

29

Explore Your Talents

Our talents are the things that we enjoy doing and are good at. Some people are good at gaming, running, speaking different languages, painting, maths or gymnastics.

Some people know their talents straight away and some only discover them when they are 30 or 40! Taking your time means you get to go on lots of adventures, make awesome mistakes and learn what you don't like doing, so you can discover what you do like doing.

ACTION: Doodle the talents that you already have or want to explore and work on. Maybe you want to be a beekeeper, gamer or learn to surf. What skills and talents could help you with this? Whatever you feel excited to learn more about could be a great talent. Add them all here!

30

My Pick Me Up Feel-Good List

Let's take time to create a feel-good list. Then, if you are having a day that doesn't feel great you can remind yourself that you have lots of ways to help yourself to feel good again. Remember that all feelings are temporary and don't last forever. This means you can change the way you feel by changing your thoughts or actions. For example, when Mello feels down, he likes to talk to a friend or go swimming to feel good again.

ACTION: This is your best list of feel-good stuff for when you need a pick me up. If you need some inspiration, you could talk to someone you trust to help you.

This is your best list of feel-good stuff for when you need a pick me up. Think about what you have around you. Maybe a comfy blanket, an ice-cold drink or spending time with your pet. Keep this list somewhere safe so you can find it to inspire yourself when you need a reminder.

1 _____

2 _____

3 _____

4 _____

5 _____

6 _____

31

Game On

If you could create the craziest game in the world, what would it be? What name would it have? Who would be in it? What would the characters be like? What would the storyline be? Would you be in it? If so, who would you be? This is your page to design any game you like!

ACTION: Doodle the characters in your game and create a great storyline. Give them speech bubbles and watch your awesome ideas come to life.

32

Celebrating Me

We all have things we can feel proud of in life. We should also remember that if we have done our best, that is good enough.

We can practise something called 'celebrating me', which means that you remind yourself of the things that you are doing well. This could be things like going to school, being kind to others, learning a new skill, being a great friend and helping at home. These are all things that you deserve to be celebrated for. When you celebrate your little and big wins every day, then you are changing your brain to feel good, be healthy and happy.

ACTION: Use this doodle sheet to add all the things that you are doing your best at. Think of the little wins and the big wins. You deserve to be celebrated and Mello is looking forward to seeing how you celebrate you.

33

My Unique Selfie

We are all 100% unique and there is no one else like us in the world! Isn't that amazing to think about! Your DNA makes you totally unique to everyone else. We also have other things that make us unique, like the colour and patterns in our eyes and the shape of our ears, the way that we speak and the thoughts that we have. The colours that we like and the things that are important to us. Some of us like to wake up early and some of us like to sleep in.

ACTION: In this doodle, take a selfie and add it to the frame. Maybe you could print this or even doodle yourself in the frame. Then look at the patterns on your thumbprint and add these. Add other things that make you who you are and unique.

89

34

Phone a Friend

Sometimes all we need is to hear is a friendly voice. This could be your grandparent, sister, friend or someone else that you miss. Sometimes just hearing a friendly voice and sharing something that is worrying you can help you to feel lighter. Sometimes they know just the right thing to say when times feel tough and speaking out the things that are on your mind can be an important step to beginning to feel stronger again.

ACTION: Who would you call when you need a friendly voice? Doodle them here so you know who to call when you need to talk. Think about what makes them so great to speak to and add that too, as well as any other doodles, shapes or colours that you want to.

35

Rainbow Food

Have you ever heard someone say 'eat the rainbow'? I mean, it would be pretty hard to actually eat a rainbow, wouldn't it, but this really means to eat a whole range of healthy foods that look like a rainbow of colours on your plate and give you different vitamins and minerals.

Happiness isn't just a mind thing, it's also a body thing, and we need the vitamins and minerals that we find in our food to have healthy minds and bodies. For example, vitamin A from milk, oranges and spinach helps us to have good eyesight and to fight infections when we aren't feeling so well. Vitamin B which we find in oats, seafood and other things helps us to get energy. So, if we are not getting our vitamins or minerals, then we can feel ill, struggle with our energy and feel down.

ACTION: Be the chef for today and design a menu or meal that has lots of colour in it because of the healthy fruits and vegetables that you add. What would this be? Maybe you will invent a new meal that no one else has thought of. Add this to your doodle. How colourful will this be?

36

The Inventor of Fun Things

If you could invent a new sport, what would it be? Think of the funny races and sports we already have, like the egg and spoon race or the wheelbarrow race. In England we have cheese rolling, toe wrestling and even worm charming, where teams of people try to charm worms out of the ground. The Zaraniq tribe in Yemen challenge each other to camel jumping to see how many camels they can jump over at once. All over the world we have extreme ironing, where people do things like parachute out of a plane while trying to iron a shirt!

ACTION: Invent your own game. Make it as bizarre and as wonderful as you like. It doesn't matter if it seems impossible; who knows what will happen in the future? Doodle your ideas on this sheet. You can add anything that you like, from words to colours to people.

37

My Story in Pictures

What would your story be if you told it in pictures? We can tell a story without words. For example, we can take pictures of things that make us smile and share them with someone. Or we can take photos when we visit a forest and help someone to experience it without even being there. What story could you tell in a day?

ACTION: Take photos throughout your day and print these. Add them to your doodle and any other words, shapes, patterns, thoughts or anything else that you would like to. Would you like to share this with someone?

38

Focus Zen

We don't often stop to notice what is around us. But stopping to appreciate what we have in our lives can help to grow happiness. It's one of the biggest happiness habits we can have!

Take a moment to look all around you. What catches your attention? What do you like about it? Or what do you notice about it? Describe the shape of something you notice to yourself. How would it feel if you touched it? What else do you notice? While you are doing this you are focusing, which is a brain super-power. When you are focusing on something and describing it, you can find little moments of joy through feeling thankful!

ACTION: Doodle what you see and what you notice. Add anything that you are drawn to adding. Maybe the shape of what you are seeing, or the colours or the patterns.

39

Sorry Is the Kindest Word

Sometimes we make mistakes and that's normal and part of being human. Making mistakes helps us to grow and learn new things. Once we make a mistake and learn from it, we often won't make the same mistake again. If we make a mistake that upsets or hurts someone in some way, then saying sorry can help us just as much as it can help the other person.

If we don't find a way to apologize when we make mistakes, then we can often get stuck in a cycle of feeling bad. Sometimes, we might want to even avoid the person, which can make us feel worse. It takes courage to apologize and when you do, then you can often start afresh.

ACTION: Is there someone you want to apologize to? How might you do that? You could bake a cake, send a kind message, write a letter or visit them. What do you think would help you to end the circle of worrying and feeling bad? Doodle your ideas here and make a plan.

40

Award of the Year

Imagine you've just won a surprise award. What could your surprise award be for? There are no rules and limits. You can create a brand-new award for anything you like. Maybe fitting the most peas ever on one spoon, the biggest splash in the pool, the funniest joke, the most bounces on the trampoline or even flying around the world on a cow! Your imagination can create anything you like!

ACTION: Add anything you like to the trophy I've doodled here. What is the title of the award? Who would give it to you? What would it look like? How would it feel to win this award?

41

My Body, My Best Friend

Have you noticed how awesome your body is at being your best friend? Your body helps you to do amazing things every day, like simply breathing, walking, swimming, laughing, eating, sleeping, moving, thinking, seeing, hearing and all of the other ways that it helps you to be you. Remember that being thankful for what we have helps to grow happiness!

ACTION: Mello is inviting you to practise some body thankfulness with him, starting by thanking every part of your body that you appreciate. For example, thank you feet, for taking me to great places! Thank you eyes, for showing me beautiful things. You can add these to your doodle bubble until you've thanked all the parts of you for being you!

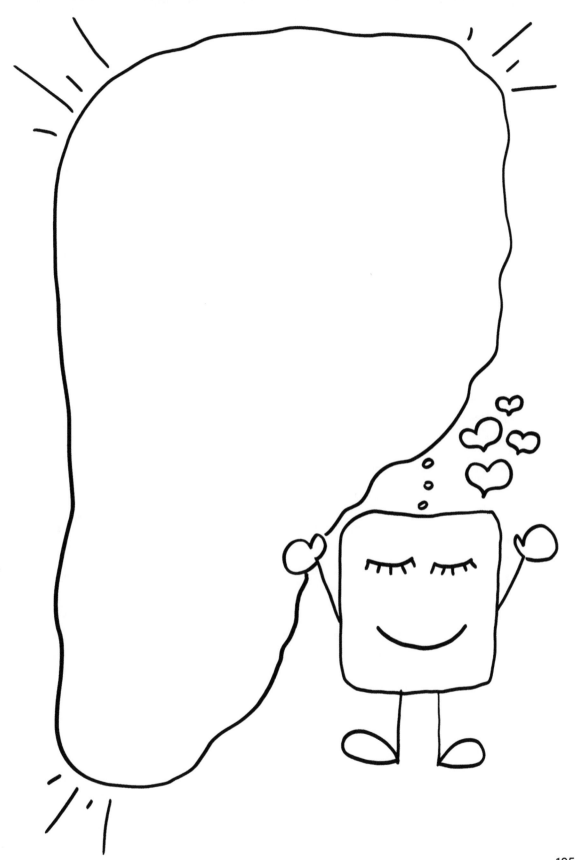

42

Invisible String

Imagine that there was an invisible string that connected you to all the places in the world that you want to visit and all the people that you want to see. Your brain can imagine things as if they were really there, so imagine away!

Using your imagination can take you on new adventures that feel exciting. That's why it's important to use your imagination to dream of the things that boost your happy feelings. If you focus too much on the things that don't feel good, you create feelings that don't feel good.

ACTION: What would your invisible string connect you to? Who would be there and where would it go around the world? What would you do there? Would you be sailing on a boat around an island or visiting someone you love? If you use your imagination, then there is no place that you can't go. Add it to the doodle!

43

Feel-Good Mood Board

When you focus on the things that you do want rather than the things that you don't want then you grow more of those feel-good feelings! When I ask people what they want they often tell me things like 'I don't want to feel unhappy'. Then I say 'Ok, but what do you want', because that's more important than what you don't want! When you give too much attention to what you don't want, you can feel down and unhappy. So this doodle is all about what you do want in your life!

ACTION: Doodle all the things that you want more of in your life. Think about people and friends, feelings and adventures. Colours, words and anything else that you want to add. You can take a picture of this and print it for your wall as a reminder or save it on your phone.

109

44

My Magic Life

We all have lots of challenges and ups and downs in our lives. There will be some days that feel harder than others. Some days will be fun and adventurous, and you will meet new people you like. Other days you might feel like the world is a little tougher. It can be helpful to remember what you do like about your life when you are having a down day. This can help you to remember that not every day is a bad day, and that good stuff is on its way to you!

ACTION: Doodle all the things that you like about your life. What will you add? Maybe your bed, your pet, the people who care about you, your hobbies, colours that you love, songs that you can play, places you have visited before, books you like to read, games you get to play and warm baths. What else will you add?

45

Be a Happiness Ninja

I know a real-life happiness ninja and her name is Marie-Claire! Her job is to spread happiness wherever she goes and she is great at it! In this doodle, I dare you to be a happiness ninja! Your dare, should you accept it, is to spread happiness wherever you go! To do this you may need to plan a little. A ninja is always prepared! You could tag a friend to help you! Who knows, you might end up starting your own Happiness Ninja Crew!

ACTION: Doodle all the ways that you could spread happiness. Make a plan that you are excited to share with others. Add patterns, colours and anything else that you want to doodle.

46

My Dreamcatcher

What are your hopes and dreams for the future? Focus on what you can control and remember that imagining what you want in your future is your first step to making it real. What could you achieve if you believed in yourself? Take a few moments now to look back over this book and see all the amazing things that you are already achieving, the wonderful ways that you are helping others around you and the gifts that you bring to this world. You are unstoppable and your future can be anything you dream it to be!

ACTION: Imagine all the things that you want to achieve in your future. Doodle the ways that you can begin to help your dreams come true. You might like to start to learn something new or grow a new skill.

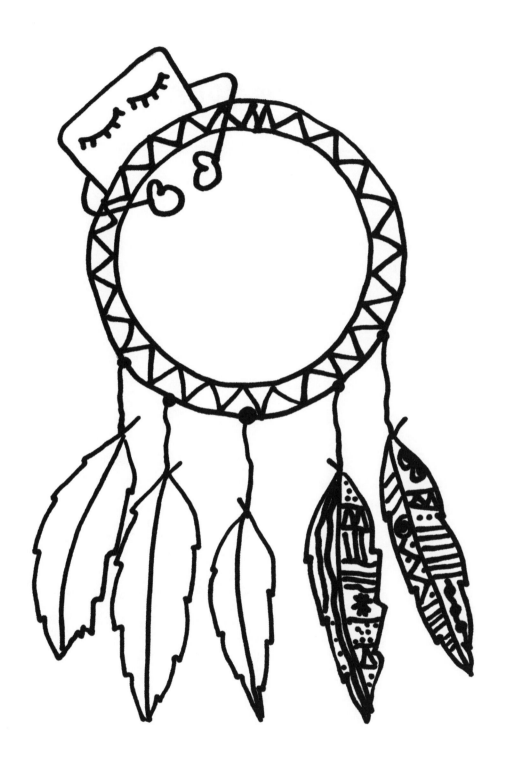

47

Super-Charge Your Happiness

As we near the end of your doodle book Mello wants to invite you to super-charge your happiness. To do this, imagine that you can take all these amazing and powerful new happiness habits and create an invisible cape of happiness! You can wear this whenever you want an extra super-charged boost of happy chemicals.

ACTION: Close your eyes and imagine an invisible cape made of the happiest feelings you have ever felt. Now imagine that you can put this on whenever you need it! What does yours look like? Create your cape as a doodle and add this to your book here!

48

My Happiness Habits

We have explored so many different happiness habits within this book. This is your space to doodle the ones that have been your favourite and have really helped you! This will become your go-to happiness list. You can come back to this list any time that you need to remind yourself of all the ways that you can take charge of your happiness.

ACTION: Doodle your favourite happiness habits here. You can flick through the book and pick out the ones that helped you most. Maybe you could take a photo of this and put it somewhere to remind you when you need a little happiness boost.

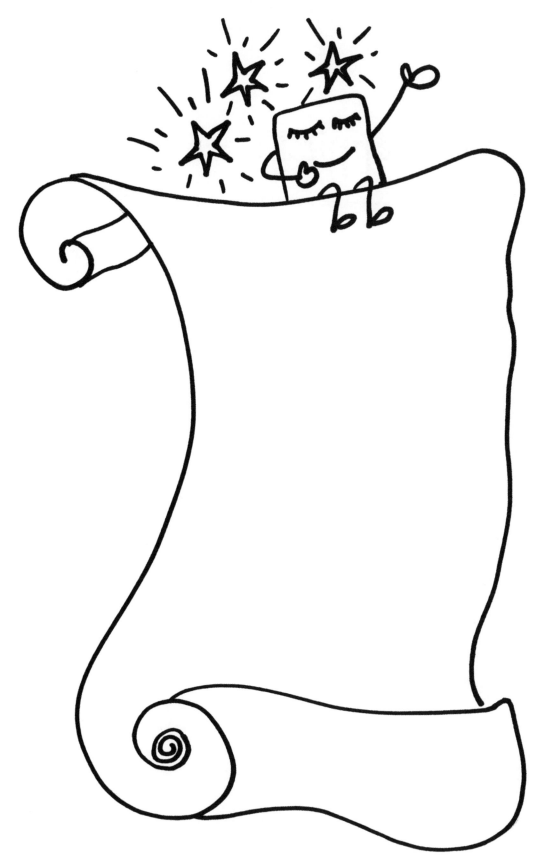

49

Your Happiest Word

At the beginning of this book, Mello invited you to create your own list of happy words. Now that you are almost at the end of your book, Mello invites you to choose one word that feels so happy that it makes you smile every time you think of it or say it out loud! You could even invent this word because this is just for you!

ACTION: Add your happy word to your thought bubble and practise saying it out loud! How happy does that make you feel? Can you save this somewhere in case you need it in the future? Maybe you could write this down on a sticky note and add it to your wall as a reminder.

121

50

Doodle Yourself Happy

Throughout this book, you have been exploring different ways that you can grow your happiness and feel-good chemicals. Now this doodle is all about seeing yourself as the happiest that you can be! Celebrate happiness and the growing spark within you!

ACTION: Close your eyes and imagine that happiness spark growing within you again and surrounding you! Now open your eyes and doodle yourself happy!

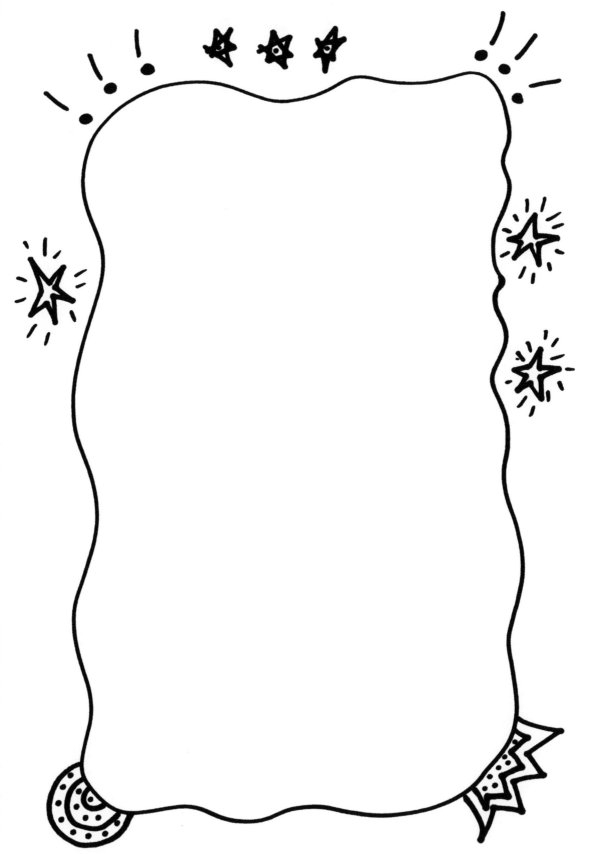

Afterword

I hope that you have loved doodling yourself happy. Now you know how to grow more happiness, remember that it is important to keep practising these habits! Just like a garden needs care, so does your happiness.

You might even like to create your own happiness space at home. A place where you can keep doodling and daydreaming new ideas.

Remember that some days will be harder than others and it's normal to feel down, because life can be tough! We have so many challenges to face, just like all the best movies, where we watch our favourite characters battling to overcome their problems. You can do this too! You are strong!

Keep talking about your feelings with others, focus on the things that help you to feel good and celebrate your wins, no matter how big or small!

Growing your happiness is an exciting adventure!

I am so proud of you for working on your happiness and I think you are awesome! You inspire me to be a happier person too!

Keep on creating!

Tanja Sharpe

Tanja Sharpe
www.tanjasharpe.com

Note

1   Chung, S.-K., Ho, F. Y.-Y. and Chan, H. C.-Y. (2022) 'The Effects of Zentangle® on Affective Well-Being Among Adults: A Pilot Randomized Controlled Trial.' *The American Journal of Occupational Therapy 76*, 5, 7605205060.